THIS MUSIC CREPT BY ME

UPON THE WATERS

The Poets' Theatre Series

ONE

Archibald MacLeish

THIS MUSIC CREPT BY ME

UPON THE WATERS

HARVARD UNIVERSITY PRESS

CAMBRIDGE, MASS.: 1953

COPYRIGHT 1953 BY ARCHIBALD MAC LEISH

FIRST EDITION

DESIGN BY JOHN HAWKES

LIBRARY OF CONGRESS CATALOG CARD NUMBER 54–5428

PRINTED IN THE UNITED STATES OF AMERICA

FOREWORD

When I published *The Fall of the City* almost twenty years ago I felt it necessary to preface the poem with yet another defense of poetry — a defense of dramatic verse for radio. Here at last, I said, was the promise of a true theatre for poets; a theatre in which the imaginative ear, not the pedantic eye, would provide the audience; a theatre in which cadence would be heard and image would be confronted and the inwardness of human action might appear: a theatre also in which poetry could regain what it cannot long exist without — a public.

Sending this new play to the printer I feel an equal compulsion to amend that declaration. I still believe in the promise but no longer in the fulfillment, at least in this country. And not only because television has, in the interim, returned the eye to its modern primacy, subordinating the unseen to the seen, but for a different reason. The theatre of which I wrote has been remodelled for more realistic purposes and there is very little hope or none at all that it will be restored to what it was, or might have been. Commercial time does not turn backwards. A few independent stations may set up tents from year to year, but Americans who wish to continue to believe that radio as a whole can be something more than a "communications industry" must look to the British Broadcasting Corporation to keep their hearts up.

What they will find there — what American writers, in any case, will find there — may make them envious but will not solve their American problems. Writers, poets, in this country are remitted, as the lawyers say, to the status quo ante — to the stage in the four-walled room. Their questions again are questions of theatre in the old sense. Where now is an American audience for poetic drama to be found? Does Mr. Eliot's resounding success on Broadway offer a hint to those, if there are any, capable of receiving it, or was the prosodic price he paid too high? Was Yeats's move in the opposite direction the right move for us, or do his chamber plays assume conditions which do not exist in the United States?

The history of the play here published will throw no light on the answer but may illuminate the problem. *This Music Crept By Me Upon The Waters* was printed in *Botteghe Oscure* in Rome in April of this year and produced, as a radio play, by Geoffrey Bridson on the

Third Program of the British Broadcasting Corporation in June. It is now about to be presented on the stage of The Poets' Theatre in Cambridge under the direction of Mary Howe. What lies beyond that, save for the fact that the BBC Third Program will produce it again this fall, I do not know. I suspect, however, that its British audience and its American audience will continue to differ in the manner suggested by the two productions.

Poets writing for the stage in this country must be, it would now appear, largely dependent on such organizations as The Poets' Theatre. They should be correspondingly grateful to those who direct these theatres, those who maintain them and those who compose their audiences. If the direction Yeats took at the end of his life is the promising direction — and it may well be — the future of poetic drama in the United States is in their hands. It is by no means a prospect to despair of, even for those who held high hopes of the stage radio might have created. Small identifiable audiences may create in time a more enduring public for poetry than the large anonymous audiences radio could have reached. And if other publishers will do what the Harvard University Press is doing in the series of verse plays here inaugurated, that public need not necessarily be small.

I should like to thank the Princess Caetani, once editor of *Commerce* and now of *Botteghe Oscure,* for her courtesy in permitting the publication of this play in book form in the United States. No one in our generation has done more than she for that never realized, never abandoned dream of a true republic of letters.

Archibald MacLeish

CONWAY, MASSACHUSETTS
SEPTEMBER 25, 1953

THIS MUSIC CREPT BY ME

UPON THE WATERS

The Antilles. A garden above the sea. Evening. Across the back of the stage and to the audience's left, the two wings of a small but elegant one-storey house: to the right, palm trees and a low wall along a cliff's edge, the sea beyond. An archway to the road outside pierces the left wall of the house. An entrance door leading to the living-room opens in the middle of the rear wall. The garden is dark except for the light of four enormous candles in hurricane lamps. Chuck Stone, his wife, Elizabeth, Oliver Oren and Alice Liam sit in long chairs half facing the low wall and the sea. Oliver is an Englishman in his late forties, the rest Americans: Alice about Oliver's age, the Stones perhaps ten years younger. They are dressed for dinner in the Caribbean fashion: the men in loose white coats, the women in cotton dinner dresses. The conversation which has been going on for some time has pretty well run out. There are empty glasses on the little tables beside the chairs.

ALICE

Who else?

ELIZABETH

Else?

ALICE

Who else is coming?
(*Elizabeth does not answer: she is looking off toward the sea.*)
Darling Elizabeth, have you forgotten?
Your dinner guests! You said the Halseys.

ELIZABETH

Yes, the Halseys.

ALICE

And who else?

OLIVER

Of course the girl's forgotten. Why shouldn't she? —
Waiting all these mortal hours!

1

ALICE

Who else besides the Halseys?

CHUCK

                                        Don't
Bother, Alice! She can't hear you.
God knows what she listens to:
Not me at least. Not on this island.

ELIZABETH

I always listen, Chuck. I hear
The sea too, that's all... and the wind.

ALICE

You love your island, darling, don't you?

CHUCK

Sometimes I think she hates it.

ELIZABETH

                                No!
Not the island.

CHUCK

                        Well, the people.

ELIZABETH

Not the island people.

CHUCK

                        No,
Not the island people! Our kind!

ELIZABETH

It isn't true I hate the island.

CHUCK

All right! You love it then!

ELIZABETH

                                I live in it.
(*There is a moment's silence.*)

OLIVER

God, will they never come? I'm starving.
It must be going on for nine.

CHUCK

It's eight.

OLIVER

                Not by the belt I buckle.

2

ALICE

People don't keep clocks in Paradise?

OLIVER

What Negro ever kept a spring
Wound in a metal box to chirp at him?
That's the white man's privilege.

CHUCK

Privilege!
You tell by constellations in your coconuts —
Or by your gullet if you've got one.
Drink, Oliver?

OLIVER

No, no more:
Not on yesterday's stomach, thank you.

CHUCK

I've known the whole American community
Fifty minutes out by clock time.

OLIVER

Have you? Extraordinary. Quite like natives.

ELIZABETH

Not the least like!

CHUCK

Fifty! Think of it!

ELIZABETH

Not the least like natives, Oliver.
They have no time to lose. They live
Now. Not late, not soon, but now.
They can't lose now. They live there.

OLIVER

Only the
Trees have found that fabulous country.

ELIZABETH

Every paradise is laid in it.
Here and now must meet each other
Like two impossible rivers joining
Just where Jerusalem begins ....
No matter which Jerusalem.

OLIVER

The unattainable, unvisited now
That's never here when we are.

3

ELIZABETH

(*violently*)

No!
Now and here together in one gulp
To burn the heart out with its happiness!

CHUCK

Elizabeth!

ELIZABETH

I'm sorry.

OLIVER

Why be sorry?
Only those who've been there know it.

ALICE

And most of them won't tell.

ELIZABETH

Sorry
Because I've never been there, then.

OLIVER

I wish your guests were now... *and* here.
Are you quite sure you asked them, darling?

CHUCK

I'm sure!

OLIVER

Ah, it's Chuck that did it.

CHUCK

The Englishman and his stomach, Oliver!

OLIVER

Why shouldn't I be hungry? Lunch —
Alice's and mine — was sandwiches
Seven thousand feet above
The empty earth — and that was water.

ALICE

Cheese what's more.

OLIVER

What's less!

ELIZABETH

Look!
It's brightening!

4

ALICE

The moon?

ELIZABETH

The moon.

OLIVER

For God's sake
Don't divert me when I'm miserable.

CHUCK

Watch these palm trees on the cliff now....

ALICE

You're like a hen in thunder, Oliver,
Brooding your addled eggs.

CHUCK

.... I planted them.
The moon, from where you're sitting, both of you,
Rises — ought to rise — just there.
I worked it out myself with almanacs.
The February moon should rise
Just in that frame of fronds precisely....
Some day this garden will be wonderful.
You wait! Another year. Two years.

ELIZABETH

Why wait? Why not delight in it now?

OLIVER

He can't. Nor you. Nor any of us.
Who was it said his whole life seemed
A preparation for what never happened?...
Like your dinner, dear Elizabeth:
A preparation for who never comes.

ALICE

How smooth the wind is. Like a river.

ELIZABETH

The always flowing of the wind....

CHUCK

They never fail, the Trades.

ALICE

It feels —
The air against my face — as though
The air were still and the earth turning.

ELIZABETH

I know. You feel the turning earth here.

ALICE

Bodies should go naked in it.

OLIVER

Not some that I can think of.

ALICE

All!
All should go beautiful in Paradise!

OLIVER

The Island Paradise! Who called it that?

CHUCK

Columbus. On the second voyage.

OLIVER

The Admiral was not precisely
Reticent was he? I remember
One of his discoveries he called
La Desirada.

CHUCK

La Désirade.
It's French now.

OLIVER

And it takes the consequences?

ELIZABETH

Quand bleuirat sur l'horizon la Désirade....

OLIVER

What's that?

ELIZABETH

Apollinaire I think:
When will the desired land-fall
Loom — grow blue — on the horizon....

OLIVER

Another of Chuck's sort, Elizabeth —
Apollinaire. The sort for whom
No voyages ever come to shore
However the sad heart prepares for it.
That's the modern poet for you!
Journeys end in no one's meeting....
But Paradise! How did he know?

CHUCK

Know what?

OLIVER

The place was Paradise?

ALICE

The Admiral?

OLIVER

The Admiral.
How did he know? It must have looked
An island much like any island.

ALICE

Maybe the Indians told him.

ELIZABETH

They might have.
Those Arawaks were cheerful creatures,
Pretty and gentle and so gay...

CHUCK

Before the Caribs ate them and the Spaniards
Relieved them of their sinful flesh
With whips and saltmines!

ELIZABETH

Old philosophers
Took them for witnesses of human innocence:
The primitive happiness of mankind.

CHUCK

What Elizabeth means — the books latched onto them.
Rousseau's Noble Savage was an Arawak.

OLIVER

Ah, that explains it all! Columbus,
Seeing those laughing, splashing Indians
Naked as jays and beautiful as children
Knew at once what latitudes he sailed in.
The place was Paradise! That settled it!
Had he no eyes at all for reefs
Or shark fins or the green volcanoes
Lurking in this smile of trees?

ALICE

They were the angels at the gate.

ELIZABETH

(*excitedly*)

I think he saw it all. And knew.

This was no island in the sea.

This was another kind of island —

A shoal in time where happiness was possible:

More perhaps than possible — inevitable.

OLIVER

Inevitable? Happiness?

ELIZABETH

Yes. Inevitable....

For those who found his island.

OLIVER

Found it!

Thousands of wanderers must have found it —

Indians, Spaniards, Negroes, Frenchmen —

Even Americans! And were they happy?

Are they? All of them? Those Negroes

Swinking half-naked in the cane?

Americans stark naked on the beaches?

ELIZABETH

Few of them have found *his* island.

OLIVER

Yes, and fewer ever will,

And fewer still return to tell of it.

Perhaps some bronze brown African woman

Lying like summer in the sun,

Languid with her mute desire,

Might turn her head and be there — might!

But who else? Your American neighbors?

If one American should see this Paradise,

Even from far off in his grog,

The way you think the Admiral saw it,

His mind would fail him! Don't deceive yourself.

We're all sleep-walkers here, Elizabeth.

You are. I am. Chuck there. Alice.

If we should find ourselves awake

Where "now" was truly now, and "here"

Just here, and nothing left to hide us,

8

We'd huddle shivering in our souls
Like those who waken in cathedrals, naked.
Oh, we'd sweat I tell you. We'd be miserable.

ELIZABETH

Some would. Some would laugh — or try to.
One or two would change their lives.

OLIVER

Would they, Elizabeth? Change? You think so?

ELIZABETH

Peter would go back to sleep.

ALICE

Peter! Peter Bolt you mean?
Is he here? On this island? Peter?
Followed you all this way?

CHUCK

                    Followed us!

ALICE

Oh, not you, Chuck.

ELIZABETH

                    Peter Bolt.
It's never now or here with Peter.
It's always somewhere else and afterward:
Afterward when the work is finished,
The fame won.

CHUCK

                    You think that's strange?
You think, because I quit and came here
Looking for — what you haven't found —
It isn't so with me too? All of us?

ALICE

What is it that you haven't found? —

ELIZABETH

What's all around us.

CHUCK

                    Is it? Is it?

OLIVER

But this not quite impetuous Peter?...

9

CHUCK

Lawyer. One of the best they tell me.
Young too. Must have heard his name.
He has a house here. God knows why:
He's never in it. One week. Two weeks.

OLIVER

Here now?

CHUCK

They're dining with us.

OLIVER

They!

CHUCK

He has a wife of course.

OLIVER

"Of course"?
That kind of wife?... Well? Isn't she?

ALICE

Elizabeth is our authority.

ELIZABETH

Authority?
Years ago I used to know him.
We haven't really talked for years.

CHUCK

Ann, my love! Not Peter: *Ann.*

ELIZABETH

No one can speak for Ann.

ALICE

Not even
Ann.

OLIVER

(*to Alice*):
You know her?

ALICE

Yes. She's beautiful.

ELIZABETH

She's everything a woman should be.

ALICE

There's nothing Ann can't do...

10

OLIVER

But?...

ELIZABETH

Feel.

ALICE

Or know she feels at least.

ELIZABETH

Or show it.

OLIVER

Patently, she's mad about him.

ALICE

Mad!
You haven't seen that smooth brown hair!

OLIVER

And he? Does he deserve her?

ALICE

Dotes on her!
Thinks of her morning noon and night!
Where is she? Is she well? Safe? Comfortable?

ELIZABETH

You think anxiety is proof of love?
It may be proof of love's disaster:
Duty doubling duty's care
Because the passionate carefulness of the heart
No longer rushes breathless....
(*Oliver flings out of his chair, paces the garden.*)

OLIVER

God!
I'm famishing. Where are these pretty people?
Do they exist? Or did Elizabeth
Dream them in that elegant head
To populate her Paradise, her island?

ALICE

Oh, they're real enough. I'd call
The J.B. Halseys real. Thick as
Porterhouses, both of them.

CHUCK

The Keoghs.

ALICE

Oliver wouldn't know the Keoghs:
They're just simple, decent people!

CHUCK

From Milwaukee.

ALICE

From Milwaukee.

OLIVER

They must be something more than simple.

CHUCK

Why?

OLIVER

To live here.

CHUCK

Why, to live here?

OLIVER

Live in this Paradise of Elizabeth's?

CHUCK

What's wrong with Paradise?

OLIVER

For saints,
Nothing.

CHUCK

For simple, decent people.
Even the decent have a right to happiness.

OLIVER

Oh, a right! You Americans
Guarantee it somewhere, don't you?
All men have a right to happiness —
You, the Keoghs, everybody.
What if happiness laid claim to them?
It might, in Paradise, you know —
People who all their lives have lived
Pursuing happiness, pursuing something
More or farther off or brighter.
In Paradise there's nothing more.
Everything that will be, is.

ELIZABETH

Is, and is everything!

OLIVER

                    They'd go mad.
We all would — all of us. We're all the same:
We live by what's still left to live for:
Something in another life,
Another love, another country,
Even in another world,
At least some other day. In Paradise
Everything is here, is this:
The ordinary heart can't bear it.
Suffering, yes: suffering we endure.
But happiness! Happiness is long ago
Or far away or not yet come to.
Only a child or those like children,
Meeting happiness in a summer's door
Can take it by the hand and run with it.
The rest walk past it and remember.

ELIZABETH

Some walk past it and forget.

OLIVER

Your island, dear Elizabeth! Your island!
It's Shakespeare's parable all over.
Enchanting music draws us through the sea,
We glimpse an inexpressible happiness,
We turn into the things we were —
A duke, his daughter, attendants, gentlemen.

ALICE

Oliver'd turn us into saints.

OLIVER

Saints of a far more rigorous discipline
Than any the meek church acknowledges.
Mexican Indians. Chinese poets.
No ordinary saint can sit
In sunlight at a door, like those
Old Negro women of Elizabeth's.
Watch your compatriots at play or mine!
Look at the Riviera! Strewn with them!
The wreckage of the right to happiness
In painted shirts and canvas trousers
Drinking Pernod before breakfast,
The possibility of Paradise so terrifies them!

ALICE

    And our compatriots here?

CHUCK

                    They drink.
    A little.

ALICE

        Chuck!

CHUCK

           All right! They drink!
    Why not? It passes time.

OLIVER

              Does it?
    Not if the place is what he called it.
    Time in Paradise never passes.
    The blessed live their lives awake.

ELIZABETH

    Each minute like the last that will be:
    Each like the first that ever was.

OLIVER

    How wise the child is all at once.

ALICE

    She's had her glimpses of the garden:
    Who hasn't?

(The brightening of the sky above the sea increases. Oliver stands with his back to it. They are silent.)

OLIVER

           Happiness is difficult.
    It takes a kind of courage most men
    Never are masters of, a kind of
    Innocent ruthlessness that lives
    Like leaves in the instant of the air:
    The courage just to be — to trust
    The wind that blows you.

ELIZABETH

             Look! The moon!
    It's rising!

OLIVER

        Do you think that fact,
    Elizabeth, deserves remark
    Just at this juncture of my discourse?

ALICE

How slow it lifts into the sky!
Look at it, Oliver! It's marvellous.

OLIVER

Dear girl, we have a moon in England.

CHUCK

Only you never see it.

OLIVER

                    Don't we!
Demure among her clouds, not strutting
Naked like that tropical piece.
Shameless the way she stares at us!

ELIZABETH

                              They say
The moon feeds on our eyes. I think
I never saw a moon more gluttonous....
I know I never saw one stranger:
So still! Silver and intent and still!
It burns like silence in a mirror.

CHUCK

Because the wind has fallen. Listen!
The Trade Wind almost never falls
Night or day — not at this season.

ALICE

I hear a kind of murmuring in the sea —
Between the slidings of the sea a syllable.

ELIZABETH

So still! So still!

ALICE

               I've never known
The world — the sea, the sky, the air —
So still.

ELIZABETH

          Nor I.

ALICE

                  The palm leaves fill
And fall as though not air but moonlight
Gathered them and let them go.
You know, it could be Paradise, it could be —
This moment anyway.

15

ELIZABETH

                It is!
If only we ourselves awoke
And trusted it, it could be. Even for
Us! If we could take it.... Dared to....

CHUCK

Take what?

ELIZABETH

              Our lives! Our lives! Our lives!
(*Elizabeth crosses to the cliff's edge, stands there looking out
to sea.*)

ALICE

Turn your face up! Close your eyes!
Feel the almost imperceptible movement
Of cool and warm across your lids
The moon makes touching you — the sliding moon.
Something unimaginably beautiful
Seems no farther from me than my hand
Could reach, if I should lift one finger.

OLIVER

Alice is giddy from her fast.

ALICE

Jeer if you please. You feel it too.
I know you, Oliver.

OLIVER

             All right, I'm giddy.
Why not? If the moon is risen
It must be — God knows what it must be —
Ten?

CHUCK

        It's half past eight.

OLIVER

              Great God!
And not a sign of them. No message.
You don't suppose this settlement of yours
Has vanished at the clap of moonlight?
Strange things happen in the wilderness.
Remember Raleigh's settlement at Jamestown?
Gone — just gone — the table set,

Food in the kitchens, and the place
Deserted. Not a soul. Perhaps
It wasn't Raleigh. Even Jamestown.

ELIZABETH

Be quiet! Listen to the sky!

OLIVER

Or those deserted ships at sea
Discovered drifting with their sails set, everything
Neat, everything in order — a child's
Toy, the captain's toddy, biscuits —
Even the cat's milk sweet and not
One single soul aboard — no explanation —
Nothing but the slapping sails,
The groaning timbers...

ALICE

                    And the little girl
Crunching popcorn in the row behind you!

CHUCK

My guess would be they stopped at Peter's
Meaning to have one drink and had
Another and, just possibly, another.

OLIVER

It isn't conceivable. I won't believe you.
People don't sit down and drink
While others hunger. No, they're gone.
Something — who knows what? — has tempted them
Past the familiar safe stockade
To those dark forests off beyond it —
God have mercy on their souls! —
Leaving the settlement uninhabited
Save for ourselves: we few remaining.

ELIZABETH

What makes you think we're safe inside,
We others? That blazing moon could burn
The whole stockade of certainty and leave us
Ignorant in the wilderness, no matter
How we'd built it out of words from home.
Where would we hide our hunger then?

17

CHUCK

Oh, for God's sake, no, Elizabeth.
I hate those games: You know I hate them.
Elizabeth is always asking
Where?... When?...

OLIVER

And you reply?

CHUCK

That's it: I don't....

ALICE

Listen!.... Listen!....
Chuck, there's something.... not the sea....

CHUCK

It's them! They're coming!

OLIVER

Ah, they're coming!
How shall we welcome them, Elizabeth? —
Sit here as though we'd finished dinner,
Smoking our cigars, and rise,
Polite in our restrained astonishment,
And wait until the boldest chirps:
"It *was* tonight, dear, wasn't it?"
And answer awfully: "It *was!*"?

ALICE

Oliver! He would! You know he would.
Don't encourage him Elizabeth.

OLIVER

You call that look encouragement?
She hasn't heard a word I've said.
(*Headlights swing across the arch: engines are cut off: voices.*)

CHUCK

Anything you want to bet
They feel no pain.

OLIVER

Those tell-tale voices!
How hideously rum reveals
The insipidity of its origins!
Liquid sugar! Listen to them!
(*Keogh opens the gateway in the arch: his wife Sally pushes past him.*)

KEOGH

God, boy, do I need a drink!

SALLY

What he means he needs another....

KEOGH

OK!

SALLY

.... little drink. He's beautiful!
The way he wears that shirt, he's beautiful!
Isn't he beautiful, Elizabeth?

KEOGH

Boy, what I've been through!

SALLY

Just beautiful!

KEOGH

Watching these goddam goofy idiots
Gawk by the water while the moon
Came up and gawked at them, for Chri'sake!
(*Helen Halsey comes through the arch: then her husband.*)

HELEN

Dear Elizabeth, forgive us!
We must be very, very late.
Peter's just behind. And Annie.

KEOGH

Behind! He hasn't left that beach.
Poor bastard's stuck there staring at it
Stiff as a jacked fish. Stiffer.

SALLY

Just
Staring at it.

CHUCK

Staring where?
What's he staring at?

SALLY

Just staring.

HELEN

Standing staring.

19

KEOGH

Wouldn't let me
Speak not even.

SALLY

Imagine that!
Not even Harry even speak!
Each of us just stood there staring.

CHUCK

Where? At what?

KEOGH

Beside the road there.

HALSEY

Where the road runs by the beach.

HELEN

The moon. We watched it rising.

KEOGH

She did!
Stopped us all beside the dune.

HELEN

No one knows how long we stood there.

KEOGH

I do. *I* know. Ask me darling.

HELEN

All of us had silver glasses.

CHUCK

Glasses?

SALLY

Silver in the moon.
Peter gave us silver glasses.

KEOGH

Keeps his cocktails in his car,
The thoughtful bastard.

HELEN

All of silver.
Oh, it was wonderful, Elizabeth.

ELIZABETH

It sounds so. Do you know each other?
This is Alice Liam, Sally:

You know Alice, Sally, don't you?
Sally Keogh, Harry Keogh...
Oliver, do you know the Halseys?
This is Oliver Oren, Helen.
Mr. and Mrs. Keogh, Oliver.

KEOGH

Colonel Keogh!

ELIZABETH

                Oh, I'm sorry.
Colonel Keogh.

KEOGH

                Not at all....
Natural error. When the wars are ended
Who remembers the poor soldiers?

HALSEY

The poor soldiers seem to, Colonel.

SALLY

Particularly colonels.

CHUCK

                  Oh
Generals remember pretty well:
Generals remember all the generals.

KEOGH

You can go to Hell, the lot of you.

ELIZABETH

Why did he stay there, Harry?

KEOGH

                     Who?

ELIZABETH

Peter.

KEOGH

        The beauty of the night!
Imagine that! At his age! Stuck there
Staring at the island in the moon
As though he'd never seen it till that moment!

OLIVER

Had he?

KEOGH

> This is his seventh year!
It wasn't only Peter either.
Know what Halsey here was saying?

HALSEY

Forget it!

KEOGH

> Don't you wish I would?
Don't you? Halsey here was saying:
"Yes!" Like that.... "Yes!".... "Yes"....
Staring at the moon-rise: "Yes!"....

HELEN

It's true. I never saw him look so —
Not even at Hyannisport that summer.
I don't know what he meant.

KEOGH

> > > Nor him:
He doesn't either.

HALSEY

> No! Forget it.

HELEN

I wish he'd looked at me like that:
Just once.

SALLY

> Like what?

HELEN

> > Oh, like a man....
Who sees the whole of his desire.

HALSEY

You don't know what you're saying, Helen.

HELEN

A man who saw his whole desire,
Near as the world was in that moon,
Might get it.

OLIVER

> Yes. And where would he be?

ELIZABETH
Here.

OLIVER

   Or his desire?

ELIZABETH

      Here.

KEOGH

They're tight as mountain ticks, the lot of them.

SALLY

They're crazy, everybody's crazy,
Craziest night I ever saw,
Like Paris, who was that was saying
Let's go crazy, dear, in Paris?
Who? We did too, we went crazy,
Just like Paris only rum,
I like rum, want to know what *I* did?
Want to know what little Sally
Did?

KEOGH

   Quiet! You're a big girl now:
You're forty-seven.

SALLY

      I kept saying,
I'm beautiful! I'm beautiful!

KEOGH

Shut up, I said. I meant it!

SALLY

      Oh,
I stood there naked by the water....
I mean....
   I stood there....
(*Silence.*)

KEOGH

      What she means
She's had one coke too many.

ELIZABETH

      Does she?
I think she means that she was beautiful!

SALLY

Elizabeth, you flatterer!

23

ELIZABETH
>
> It isn't flattery.
> Why are you frightened to remember?

SALLY
>
> I'm not!

ELIZABETH
>
> You are. You'd rather think
> What Harry thinks — that you were drunk —
> Than know what you knew then.

SALLY
>
> Elizabeth!
> I don't know what you mean.

ELIZABETH
>
> I think you
> Do.... or did.
> *(There is an awkward silence.)*

CHUCK
>
> Let's go indoors:
> The Bolts will be along. We'll have
> That drink the Colonel needs indoors.

KEOGH
>
> And how he needs it!

OLIVER
>
> Poor dear Alice,
> Tottering for lack of food.

ALICE
>
> I thought
> You'd fainted, Oliver. I couldn't hear you.

SALLY
>
> I want Elizabeth to answer me.
> Elizabeth has made me cry....
> I don't know why she did.

ELIZABETH
>
> It isn't
> You. It's all of us. We face our lives
> Like young girls in a gallery of mirrors.
> Some glittering, unexpected moment
> Shows us our images and we shriek

With childish, hysterical laughter, caught
Naked in the simplicity of ourselves....
You needn't stare at me. You know it — all of you.

HELEN

Dear Elizabeth! It's the island!
People say things on an island —
Things they never meant to say:
They feel so far off....

ELIZABETH

Yes, and see
Things they never meant to see
And tell themselves they've never seen them!
We shouldn't live here, any of us.
We're out of place in so much light!
The green volcano in those hills
Could drown us in a flood of fire
And we'd go under giggling.

CHUCK

Sweet
Love! How violent you are!

ELIZABETH

Go in. I'll follow you. Please go.
Forgive me.

CHUCK

Come and get it!
(*From the door*)
Ice
Cold! Coals of ice!
(*They straggle in, awkwardly and rather self-consciously.
Elizabeth walks to the cliff's edge over the sea and stands
leaning against a palm trunk. The headlights of a car sweep
the archway against the moon and are switched off. Snatches
of phonograph music drift out over the sound of the sea, and,
occasionally, voices.*)

KEOGH (*off*)
God that's good! What did he call it?

HALSEY (*off*)
Coals of ice.

ALICE (*off*)
Elizabeth's volcano.

SALLY　　*(off)*
Elizabeth's volcano!

CHUCK　　*(off)*
　　　　　　　　　　Right! Where is she?
Elizabeth!
(He comes to the door calling)
　　　　　Elizabeth!

HELEN
　　　　　　　　Don't pester her.
(In the door beside him)
Even hostesses must have their moments.

CHUCK

What a woman of the world you are.

HELEN

Your world, Chuck?

CHUCK
　　　　　　　　And what a woman.
You smell like almonds. Only warmer.

HELEN

Don't! Please don't! Oh, I know
It's nothing to us — either of us:
Just the usual salute. It isn't
That....

CHUCK
　　　　　What is it, then?

HELEN
　　　　　　　　　　　It's me:
I don't know who I am. I don't
Know!

CHUCK
　　　　　You want a man should show you?

HELEN

Please! I mean it Chuck. I heard
Something that frightened me beside the water.
There wasn't any sound at all —
No sound at all and yet I heard
Ravishing laughter on the sea
Like negresses: in love they say
They shriek with laughter.... it was horrible!

26

I stood there staring at the moon and heard
Ravishing laughter on the water....
I don't know what I am, I don't know....

HALSEY   (*off*)
Pull the door shut, will you?

HELEN

                        ... anything.

HALSEY

The Colonel hates the moon....
(*Chuck and Helen turn back into the room pulling the door
to. Peter and Ann Bolt enter through the archway. Peter stops
in the blazing moonlight in the garden turning away from the
door and the chatter of voices.*)

ANN

Peter, we're terribly late. Please come.

PETER

You go. I need time.... It takes
Time.

ANN

         What does? What takes time?
I don't understand you, Peter.
What takes time? You've changed so.

PETER

                         Have I?
I wish I knew I had.

ANN

         Peter!
You don't — can't — mean that, Peter!

PETER

Changed into something that can live.

ANN

Live!

PETER

      Live here. Live in this island.

ANN

You couldn't bear it. Not the island.
Not a night like this. I know you:
Oh, my dear, how well I know you.

27

You need to earn your life to live in it
Even though the earning cost you
All your lifetime and yourself.
I know those obstinate hounds you ride to.
I hear them whimpering in your sleep
Night after night.

PETER

                    For Christ's sake, Annie!
I said — if there were words to say it....

ANN

Tell me. Try to tell me, Peter.

PETER

I said that what I suddenly understood
There in the moonlight, on the beach, was —
This is what it *is*! Just this! —
Not something afterward or elsewhere.
You live it or you don't, but what you
Live or don't live is just this:
This, this moment now, this moon now....
This man here on an island watching.
(*He turns away from her.*)
I understood it as you understand
A knife blade driven in your side:
The way you understand in dreams
That waken in a giddiness of certainty.

ANN

That passes when you waken.

PETER

                        Yes!
Yes! God, Annie, you're so sensible!

ANN

I saw the moon too, rising.

PETER

                   You?....
All my life I've lived tomorrow
Waiting for my life to come:
Promises to come true tomorrow,
Journeys to begin tomorrow,
Mornings in the sun tomorrow,
Books read, words written,

All tomorrow. Cities visited.
Even this fever of the sleepless heart
Slept away tomorrow.... all of it.

ANN

Truth to be told at last .... tomorrow.

PETER

We cling so to the skirts of suffering
Like children to their mothers — hold
The hand that hurts our hand for fear
We'll lose ourselves unless it hurts us! —
Making a virtue of our cowardice:
Pretending that a sense of sin and shame
Is holier than the happiness we fumble.

ANN

What is it that you have to do?

PETER

To do?

ANN

What is it?

PETER

I don't know.

ANN

And so there is.... is something, Peter?

PETER

I need to know the thing I know.
I need to think a little.

ANN

Yes.
I'll go. Come when you can.

PETER

I promise.

ANN

Promise! If we only could....
(*Ann opens the door of the house, there is a burst of voices.*)

CHUCK   (*off*)
There they are!

SALLY   (*off*)
There *she* is!

29

KEOGH *(off)*

                                        Where's
Peter for the love of God?

ANN

(going in)

                                        Coming.
He's coming. Do forgive us, Chuck....
Elizabeth.... Where is she?.... all of you.
(The door closes. Elizabeth comes into the moonlight.)

PETER

Elizabeth!

ELIZABETH

                        I didn't mean to startle you.
The rest of them went in. I couldn't.

PETER

We're dreadfully late. It's all my fault.
I'm sorry.

ELIZABETH

                        Don't be. Island chickens
Cook forever without noticing:
All you need to do is baste them.
Island diners baste themselves.

PETER

You heard?

ELIZABETH

                        I couldn't help it.

PETER

                                   When the wind
Fell and that sudden silence of the moon
Touched everything....

ELIZABETH

                                   With silver....

PETER

                                             Yes,
With silver.... where were you?

ELIZABETH

                                        Beside
The palms there at the little table —
Alice and Oliver and Chuck and I.

PETER

I was on that beach beside the water
Drinking — I don't know — making drinks,
Talking the usual idiotic nonsense,
Thinking nothing at all: certainly
Nothing that would change a life....
And you? You too? Beside that palm tree?

ELIZABETH

As though I'd started out of sleep.

PETER

Yes. As one would start from sleep.
I stood and I was *there*! As though
I'd turned a corner suddenly and come —
I don't know where but come there. Oh,
As though I'd ended and begun.

ELIZABETH

                      I know.

PETER

Even the glass between my fingers
Glittered in that fiery silent moon
And such a surge of happiness went over me
Everything was possible.

ELIZABETH

                   I thought of
You.

PETER

      Only when I thought of you —
Only then did that inexplicable happiness
Take form and meaning and grow capable....

ELIZABETH

                                Of breath.

PETER

Of breath.

ELIZABETH

       It's strange.

PETER

            It's very strange
After all these years of silence.

ELIZABETH

Perhaps we've known too long in silence
Ever to find voices now.
We've kept our questions in the dark so deep
Like prisoners that they have no voices.

PETER

And yet they've learned to speak.

ELIZABETH

But how?

PETER

Who knows? The moon rose and the time was
Now.

ELIZABETH

Happiness was always now.
Happiness is real — the only
Real reality that any of us
Ever have glimpses of. The rest —
The hurt, the misery — all vanishes,
Only the blinding instant left us.

PETER

Why does it take so long to know?
We tell our miserable creeping hearts
Men aren't made for happiness.

ELIZABETH

The world is.

PETER

I never knew it till tonight.

ELIZABETH

This world is. And we two in it.

PETER

Answerable to the loveliness of our lives:
To nothing else.

ELIZABETH

To nothing else.
(*They touch each other.*)

PETER

Removed by some enchantment not of change
To this... this instant.... this forever....
Never to go back.

ELIZABETH

No! Never!

PETER

Promise me.

ELIZABETH

I promise you.... If we should turn
Even our hearts to look behind us....

PETER

Even our hearts would turn to salt.
Come!

ELIZABETH

Where?

PETER

No matter where.
Anywhere but through that door....

ELIZABETH

And back.

PETER

And back.
(*They cross to the archway. Elizabeth stops in the gate.*)

ELIZABETH

There's wind again.
Look! The clouds have crossed the moon.

PETER

Hurry! Hurry!
(*The house door blows open in a gust of wind. The voices rise.*)

CHUCK

(*off, shouting*)
Soup's on! Soup's on!

KEOGH

(*off, singing*)
Dinner's over: supper's cookin'
Old Dan Tucker just stand there lookin'....

PETER

That's my car there. Can you see?
Wait, I'll pull the gate shut.

ELIZABETH (*off*)

Come!

HELEN

(*in the door*)
Elizabeth was in the garden, wasn't she?
There they are. There's Peter anyway.
Where's your Annie, Peter?

SALLY

(*in the door*)
                              Where's
Annie?

HELEN

          Can't you hear me, Peter?

KEOGH

(*in the door*)
Old Dan Tucker just stand there lookin'....

SALLY

The wind is up. He doesn't hear us.
Peter, Peter. Where's Annie, Peter?

PETER

(*the gate still open*)
She's in the house.

HELEN

                    She isn't though.
She came and looked and vanished.

SALLY

                              Looked!
She didn't even look. She stood there
Smiling at the floor — just smiling.
When I spoke to her she was gone.
(*Oliver, Alice, Halsey and Keogh come out into the garden.*)

OLIVER

A miracle, my friends, has happened.
Dinner has been announced. It may be,
After such protracted suffering,
The word conveys no meaning. Dinner!

SALLY

Peter, they saw her on the cliff.

PETER

The cliff?

HELEN

          She's not there now.

PETER

                         What cliff?

SALLY

Outside that window of Elizabeth's
Where everything pitches off into the sea.
There's not five feet of level rock
Between the window sill and....

KEOGH

                         Listen!
What are you telling the poor guy!
Ann's all right. She always will be.

HALSEY

Of all the women in God's world
Ann would be the last to....

SALLY

                    What?
Go on and say it!

KEOGH

                You goddam girls!
You make my tooth ache where it shouldn't.
You're acting like a pair of mischievous,
Wild, half-witted, crazy children
Trying to terrify yourselves
By scaring all of us.

SALLY

               Drop dead!
And not from any cliff top either:
Just drop!

HALSEY

        Sally!

SALLY

           All right! —
"Sally!" What's got into everybody?
You know the cliff as well as I do.
There's one way out: it's through the room.

OLIVER

She might have come and we not noticed.
Those coals of ice of Chuck's demand
The most meticulous concentration.

SALLY

I leaned across the cliff's edge, looking.
There wasn't anything at all — not anything.
Only the moonlight on those black
Enormous surges when they shattered:
They say they come from Africa, those surges.

KEOGH

I swear to God I'll beat you, Sally.
(*Peter turns toward the door of the house, walks a few steps,
runs. The door swings in the wind after him.*)

HELEN

He doesn't believe you, gentlemen.

SALLY

                                          Why should he?
Some things you have to see yourself.

KEOGH

You mean the things that haven't happened!
(*Elizabeth has come back through the gate. They do not see
her.*)

HELEN

How can you know they haven't happened?

HALSEY

Not by looking in the sea
For dead girls' bodies!

HELEN

                           I think you're heartless,
Both of you! Heartless! Heartless!

ELIZABETH

                              Helen!
What is it, Helen?

HELEN

                        Oh, Elizabeth:
It's Annie....

SALLY

                 Annie's gone. She's gone.

HELEN

They saw her on the cliff....

HALSEY

Be quiet!
Will you be quiet, both of you?

ELIZABETH

Where's Peter?

SALLY

He's gone to look for her.

ELIZABETH

Gone back?

SALLY

Back?

ELIZABETH

It doesn't matter. Gone.

KEOGH

The whole thing's
Nonsense! Peter knows its nonsense.
(*Peter comes slowly out of the door of the house.*)

SALLY

All right — Ask him! There he is.

PETER

She's in the kitchen. Cooking.

OLIVER

Bless her!

PETER

Something went wrong with the potatoes.

KEOGH

There you have it, Sal, God damn you!

SALLY

Kiss me, I forgive you, darling.

OLIVER

Bless the woman! The potatoes!
(*Elizabeth has begun to laugh, a high, clear, sudden peal that turns into an hysterical sobbing sound and breaks off. Peter crosses to the wall above the sea.*)

HELEN

Nothing has happened. It's all right.

37

ELIZABETH

    I know.

HELEN

         Nothing. Nothing at all.
(The door opens. Chuck is standing there with a cocktail shaker in his hand.)

CHUCK

    Supper's over: breakfast's cooking.

OLIVER

    Shall we break bread?

ELIZABETH

              At least there's bread —
And salt.

OLIVER

      And Ann's potatoes.

ELIZABETH

             Yes,
And Ann's potatoes. Are you coming, Peter?
(They go in. The door is pulled shut. There is the same chatter of indistinguishable voices over the playing of the phonograph. The moon, clear of the rushing clouds, shines white and still on the house front and the garden.)

CURTAIN